# Harry the Fly

## Question Guide

## Tanya Popovski

Published by PoP-O Books 2019
Copyright © 2019 Tanya Popovski

www.popobooks.com.au

Copying of this book for educational purposes: All rights reserved. No part of this publication may be reproduced, stored in a retrieval system, or transmitted in any form or by any means, electronic, mechanical, photocopying, recording or otherwise, without the prior written permission from the publisher.

A catalogue record for this book is available from
the National Library of Australia.

Book cover design and formatting services by BookCoverCafe.com

First edition 2019

ISBN 978-0-6484160-2-9

# Contents

| | |
|---|---|
| Getting Started | 1 |
| Tips for Using the Question Guide | 3 |
| Comprehension Strategies | 5 |
| Title page | 7 |
| Page Three | 9 |
| Page Four | 11 |
| Page Five | 13 |
| Page Six | 15 |
| Page Eight | 17 |
| Page Ten | 19 |
| Page Eleven | 21 |
| Page Twelve | 23 |
| Page Thirteen | 25 |
| Page Fourteen | 27 |
| Page Fifteen | 29 |
| Words and Phrases Used in Chronological Order | 31 |

# Getting Started

Kindergarten and year-1 reading expectations are quite different to those of mid to upper primary. In the early years, the focus is on decoding (learning how to read using symbols, sounds, sentences, and visual features). As the reader moves through the grades, the focus of reading in the classroom is about making meaning. The reader is then taught skills to deepen their understanding in order to read to learn.

The chosen book should be at a level below the reader's reading level. If you judge that the text is too difficult for the reader, choose a book at a lower level. This will allow the reader to concentrate on the meaning of the story, thereby encouraging higher-order thinking.

There is no need for pre-reading since a competent reader at this level will be able to read the text. The book should not be read in one sitting. Ask the comprehension questions after the reader has finished the text on each page. Continue to do this for approximately fifteen to twenty minutes. It is acceptable to take more than two sessions to complete questioning of the story. Go at the pace of the reader.

# Tips for Using the Question Guide

The symbol ✪ indicates that an explanation for the word or phrase used can be found in the list at the back of this guide, which you can refer to for further clarification.

This book should not be seen as a text but rather a conversation of learning. When you have asked the reader each comprehension question, give them time to think before responding. The answers have been provided so you can give the reader the answer, which becomes a teachable moment.✪

If the reader has limited experience with a particular concept, take the opportunity to explore it further through the use of other resources (books, internet, etc). To use *Stop Annoying Me* as an example, if the reader has no understanding of the way a bull behaves, the words 'raging bull' will have no meaning. In this instance, you could take a moment to explain.

The answers provided in the *Question Guide* are general, and are given as examples only of acceptable answers. If the reader's answer is not relevant to the text, or cannot be justified with evidence from the text, this becomes a teachable moment. Give the answer, and show how you worked it out. The reader's responses do not have to cover all of the suggested answers.

If the reader's prediction of the title is not relevant to the clues on the page, avoid correcting their prediction straightaway. Instead, wait until they have finished reading the story to address the initial prediction. For example, you could say: 'At the beginning of the story, you predicted that the title would be [*repeat the reader's initial prediction*]. Now that you've read the story, how accurate do you think your prediction was? What clues could you have used on the title page to help you predict more accurately?'

The superscript numbers at the end of the questions relate to the tracking sheets (purchased separately at www.popobooks.com.au) and are linked to the Australian Curriculum.

# Comprehension Strategies

Good learners draw on a range of comprehension strategies to deepen their understanding of written text. The *Question Guide* has been intentionally formulated to use the six comprehension strategies to explicitly teach how we understand texts. They are colour coded, with each colour corresponding to one of the six strategies.

**Making connections** Learners make connections with self, text and what is happening in the world.

**Predicting** Good readers use the information from illustrations, text and experiences to predict what will be read.

**Questioning** Good readers clarify meaning and aim for a deeper level of understanding by posing and answering questions.

**Monitoring** Good readers know what to do if something in the text doesn't make sense.

**Visualising** Good readers bring text to life by creating mental pictures from what they are reading.

**Summarising** Good readers are able to locate the most important ideas in a text and retell them in their own words.

# Title page

Allow the reader to read the title and look at the illustration.

Who do you think this story could be about?[1]
Reader to give a personal response

What facts do you already know about flies?[2]
Various responses

What is your attitude towards flies? How do you feel about them?[3]
Reader to give a personal response

Hello, my name is Harry and I'm sure we have met before. You probably know me as a common housefly, but my scientific name is *Musca domestica*.

I love to fly around your home, and sometimes when I find a mirror I stop to have a good look at myself.

# Page Three

Allow the reader to read the text aloud.

What is the meaning of the term *Musca domestica*?[8]
It's the scientific name for a common housefly.

What is a 'scientific' name?[17]
'Scientific' is a word used by scientists. Scientific names usually come from Latin or Greek.

Who is telling this story?[9]
Harry

What do you think Harry sees when he looks in the mirror?[4]
Suggestions: wings, legs, eyes; any body parts

This text has some fact and some fiction. Can you identify the different types of information?[12]
Fact: common housefly, *Musca domestica*
Fiction: Harry looks in the mirror, Harry introduces himself

I love my wings. I have two sets. The main pair helps me to fly, and the smaller pair keeps me balanced so I don't wobble when I'm buzzing through the air.

## Page Four

Allow the reader to read the text aloud.

What is the text describing?[11]
The fly's wings

What information does the text give you about the fly's wings?[8]
- A fly has two sets of wings.
- The main pair of wings assists with flying, and the smaller pair of wings keeps the fly balanced.

How does the illustration add to this information?[14]
The illustration helps by giving a visual image of the written description, assisting the reader to visualise accurately.

My tongue is shaped like a straw, and I use it to slurp up my food.[RW100]

# Page Five

Allow the reader to read the text aloud.

➤ A housefly uses its tongue like a straw. What can you infer✪ from this about the fly's food?[11]
Solid food is broken down into liquids. (The fly is able to do this by using digestive juices from its stomach.)

How do the illustrations support the text?[19]
The part of the fly being discussed is magnified in the illustration.

What is onomatopoeia?✪
Onomatopoeia is when a word mimics the sound of an object or action when it is pronounced (e.g. bang, moo, jingle).

Can you think of some words that are onomatopoeia?[17]
Suggestions: bang, moo, jingle, cuckoo, splash, roar

Can you identify the onomatopoeia in the text?[15]
Slurp

What does it mean to slurp?[17]
Slurp: to eat or drink something making a loud sucking noise

And just look at my beautiful eyes. Did you know that flies' eyes are the most complicated in the insect world?

They're called compound eyes, which means they're made up of many repeating units called ommatidia. Having ommatidia means I can detect the smallest of movements that other creatures may miss. I use my feet to rub my eyes clean because I don't have eyelids like you do.

## Page Six

Allow the reader to read the text aloud.

If the facts from the last three pages had a subheading in a factual book, what might it be?[13]
The Fly's Body

What is the purpose of a question in the text?[18]
A question is used for effect. It draws the reader's attention to that particular fact.

What is the meaning of the word 'detect'? Can you try to work it out from the context (from within the sentence or part of the story in which the word is written)?[17]
Detect: to discover or notice

When does an apostrophe go after the –s in a word?[18]
Generally, if the noun ✪ (which is a part of speech ✪) is plural ✪ the apostrophe goes after the *-s*.
The witches' broom (witches is plural)
The witch's broom (witch is singular)

Why is 'detecting the smallest of movements' helpful to a fly?[11]
It can avoid being swatted, or eaten by a predator.

What are you visualising as you read this text?[7]
Harry looking into a mirror, focusing on his eyes
Harry cleaning his eyes
Harry moving quickly at the smallest of movements

How does a fly clean its eyes?[8]
It rubs its feet over its eyes because it has no eyelids.

What are some new facts you have learnt so far?[8]
The word 'ommatidia' means made up of repeated cells.
A fly has the most complicated eyes in the world.
Flies rub their eyes with their feet to clean them.

As I buzz around, landing on anything and everything, I can carry up to 33 million diseases from plants, animals or bacteria. This means that you need to be careful when I'm around. It's especially important that you are hygienic and wash your hands before you eat. You might not have seen me, but I could have landed on your desk, pen or bag when you weren't looking.

# Page Eight

Allow the reader to read the text aloud.

What does the word 'hygienic' mean? Can you try to work it out from the context (from within the sentence or part of the story in which the word is written)?[16]
Hygiene: the practice of keeping clean to stay healthy and prevent disease

Why would we need to be careful if Harry was around?[8]
He could carry up to 33 million diseases, and if he landed on your food or things that you use you could become sick.

Why is it suggested that it is important to be hygienic?[12]
You could pick up germs from a fly, and if you touched your food and then ate it, it could make you sick.

Think of two words that are not in the text that reflect your thinking about the text.[21]
Various responses
Examples: spreading, clean
Flies spread diseases because they can land on anything. You might think your hands are clean, but a fly may have landed on something you have touched so it is important to wash your hands before you eat.

It's not all bad, I can help the police solve murders. People who study insects like me are called entomologists. These scientists are able to tell when a death has taken place just by looking at insects at the scene. My friends and I are proud to be an important part of that process.

# Page Ten

Allow the reader to read the text aloud.

### What is an entomologist?[8]
Entomologist: A person who studies insects

### We know that entomologists study flies, but which other insects do they also study?[13]
Insect: a very small animal with a hard covering over its body; most insects have three pairs of legs, and one or two pairs of wings (e.g. beetle, cricket, bee, ant, butterfly, mosquito, ladybird, flea, wasp)

### According to the text, how do flies help the police?[8]
Flies can help to solve murders. By studying insects at the scene, entomologists can work out the time of death.

### Who is being referred to in the words 'my friends and I'?
Flies and insects

Flies are also very useful to doctors. Baby flies, also known as maggots, can be used to help people who have injuries to their flesh. These clever maggots eat the damaged flesh and this helps the wound to heal.

For example, doctors might use the help of baby flies with someone who has been badly burnt.

## Page Eleven

Allow the reader to read the text aloud.

▶ What are maggots?[8]
Baby flies

Are there any words you are unsure about?
If the answer is no, ask:
▶ What is the base word ✪ of 'injuries'?
Injury
What is an injury? Can you use it in a sentence?
Injury: damage that causes pain (e.g. The footballer suffered an injury when he was tackled).

▶ How could maggots help someone who has a burn injury?[8]
The maggots would eat the damaged flesh and help the wound to heal.

Choose three key words to help you retell the information.[22]
Various responses
Examples: doctors, maggots, flesh
Flies help doctors. Maggots are used to eat the flesh of wounds to help them heal.

I once heard that you think flies are pests. How could you think that, after all we do? We help the environment by breaking down food waste and it only takes us a couple of days. We pollinate flowers, control other pests, and provide food for birds and fish. Would a pest do all those good things?

# Page Twelve

Allow the reader to read the text aloud.

How has the author conveyed (shown) Harry's attitude?[24]
The author has written the text as though Harry is having a conversation with the reader. Harry can't believe that people think he is a pest. He is upset and annoyed.

Why does Harry ask questions?[11]
To emphasise the information by making you think about it

In what way are you effected by the last question?[18]
It makes you think about all the good things that flies do.

In the beginning you told me how you felt about flies. How do you feel about flies now, and why?[5]
Various responses
Reader to refer to the text to justify response

# Page Thirteen

Allow the reader to read the title and look at the illustration.

Why do the illustrations show Harry as a hero?[14]

The illustrator has drawn Harry as a hero because there are many things that flies do to help society.

Name some things that would make flies heroes.[12]

- Help to solve murders
- Help people who have injuries to their flesh
- Break down food waste in a few days
- Pollinate flowers
- Control other pests
- Provide food for birds and fish

Doing all this work has made me quite tired. I think I'll go and sit in my favourite spot out of the wind.

## Page Fourteen

Allow the reader to read the text aloud.

Where is Harry going to get out of the wind?[10]

On the bin

What information helps you to infer this information?[19]

The illustration gives us visual information about what flies do. Personal experience and knowledge (making connections) also helps.

Why would a bin be a favourite place for Harry?[10]

It's out of the wind and he can eat the leftover food.

So the next time you see me buzzing around and want to swat me, stop for a moment and think about all the good that flies do.

# Page Fifteen

Allow the reader to read the text aloud.

Compare this book to a nonfiction book about flies (or any other informative text you're familiar with). How has the author presented this information differently?[6]

A narrative tells a fictional (made-up) story. This text is similar to a narrative because it has a main character, Harry, but it also gives you factual information about a fly.

Judging from what you have now learned about flies, how important do you think they are? Justify (provide a reason for) your answer.[22]

- They assist medically
- They help to solve murders
- They help the environment by breaking down food waste
- They pollinate flowers
- They control other pests
- They are a food source for birds and fish

If you were writing this text, what would be the main thing you would want the reader to think about?[28]

Flies may be pests to some people and spread diseases, but they also do a lot of good.

If you were to talk about this book with a friend, what would you say?[3]

Various responses

Has the technique used to write this book helped you as a reader? If so, how has it helped? If not, why hasn't it helped?[25]

Possible responses:

It's interesting because it's written differently to an informative text.

When someone is talking to you, you usually listen.

It's difficult to know what is true or not true (fact or fiction).

How could we ensure/verify that the factual information in this book is accurate?[20]

Read or research other sources of information about flies.

# Words and Phrases Used in Chronological Order

**teachable moment** An unplanned opportunity that arises in the classroom where the teacher has an ideal chance to offer insight to their students; not something that can be planned for; a fleeting opportunity that must be sensed and seized by the teacher. If the reader is unable to answer the question, answers the question incorrectly, or after prompting is still unsure, take the opportunity to tell them the answer and show them how you reached that conclusion.

**infer** When you use clues from the story to figure out something that the author doesn't tell you. Using facts, observations and reasoning to come up with an assumption or conclusion (e.g. *The ground was wet and the leaves were moving around.* Inference: It had been raining and it was windy. *On Jocelyn's return from her holiday, her plants were limp and droopy.* Inference: Her plants had not been watered during the time that she was away.)

**onomatopoeia** Onomatopoeia is when a word mimics the sound of an object or action when it is pronounced (e.g. *grunt*, *swish*, *buzz*, *beep*, *slosh*, *tick*, *zap*).

**part of speech** In the English language, each word has elements with unique meanings. Based on how we use words and their functions, they are categorised into parts of speech. There are eight major parts of speech: noun, pronoun, verb, adverb, adjective, conjunction, preposition and interjection.

| Part of Speech | Definition | Examples |
| --- | --- | --- |
| Noun | A word that names a person, place, thing or condition | cat, dog, man, Wollongong, cough, virus |
| Pronoun | A word that can take the place of a noun or noun phrase | I, it, she, mine, his, hers, we, they, theirs, ours |
| Verb | An action word | think, imagine, hit, run, walk |
| Adverb | A word that describes actions; also describes other descriptive words | daily, fairly, calmly, jealously |
| Adjective | A word that describes a noun or pronoun | a beautiful boy, a majestic swan |
| Conjunction | A word that connects other words, phrases, clauses or sentences | and, while, because |
| Preposition | Refers to words that specify location, or a location in time | above, below, throughout, outside, before, near, since |
| Interjection | Words that express emotions | ouch, hooray, hey, hurry |

**plural** An amount greater than one (e.g. **ten apples**).

**reflect your thinking** When the reader is asked to choose two words to reflect their thinking, they should be words that reflect the whole of the text selection and not two words literally lifted from the text. This may take some time and prompting because it requires analysing, generating and integrating the levels of thinking. If two words are chosen directly from the text, take the opportunity to teach this strategy explicitly by using the example provided.

**base word** A base word is a part of a word that cannot be broken down, giving the word its basic meaning. Sometimes base words have letters added to the beginning and end of the word. A base word is also referred to as a root word.

|  | Base Word |
| --- | --- |
| fastest | fast |
| magical | magic |

Learn with

www.ingramcontent.com/pod-product-compliance
Lightning Source LLC
Chambersburg PA
CBHW062106290426
44110CB00022B/2732